Poetry & Artwork of Sex, Love & Relationships

The Art of Raw Desire

First published in Australia by HiveMind Productions LLC, 2020.

Copyright © HiveMind Productions, 2020.

Jae West has asserted her moral right under the Copyright Act 1968, [2006], and Patents Act 1990, to be identified as the author of this work.

All rights reserved. No reproduction, copy or transmission of this publication may be made without written permission. No paragraph of this publication may be reproduced, copied or transmitted save with written permission or in accordance with the provisions of the Copyright Act 1968, [2006]. Any person who does any unauthorised act in relation to this publication may be liable to criminal prosecution and civil claims for damages.

ISBN: 978-0-6489108-9-3

Typeset/Cover Design by – HiveMind Productions.
Artwork – Kate Gillett @kate.gillett

Poetry & Artwork of Sex, Love & Relationships

The Art of Raw Desire

by

Jae West

Artwork by Kate Gillett

The Art of Raw Desire

Contents

Devotion	2
Raw Desire	6
Dreaming	8
Magic Moments	10
Rebirth	12
The Authentic You	14
Contemplation	18
Stardust	22
Crazy About You	26
Beautiful Mess	28
Rainbows	32
Forbidden Fruit	36
Tremble	40
Claim	42
Green Eyes	44
Dawn Break	46
Inhale. Exhale.	48
Rainclouds	52
Shipwreck	54
Completion	56
Wings	58
Grey	60
I Choose You	64
What If	66
Vows to Oneself	70

Poetry & Artwork of Sex, Love & Relationships

The Art of Raw Desire

Poetry & Artwork of Sex, Love & Relationships

devotion

I can feel your stare of desire, but what of devotion?
I can hear I'm the one you admire, but in every emotion?
Will you withstand the storm, when I'm wild and furious?
Then let me explore when I'm cheeky and curious?
When I'm lost and bewildered will you bring me back home?
Remind me of the truth that I'm never alone
Will you hold me in the deepest sadness, when I've completely lost faith
Will you guide me to my heart to help me feel safe
When I fall to pieces, will you be a boy or a man?
When I run from your love, will you leave or stand?
Can I trust in your word with full accountability?
or will you flee from the pressure of your own responsibility?
Will you know the difference between my wants and my needs?
Will you feel when help is needed or when it impedes?
When I'm out of place, will you speak up or stay silent?
When I ask for too much, will you stay firm or compliant?
Will you do right your wrongs when you make mistakes?
Will you speak your truth even if your voice shakes?
Will you run at the first sign of defeat?
Or will you love and adore me until we're complete?
Will you choose me and simultaneously remind me I'm free?
Show me the meaning of vulnerability
Will you help me let go of unneeded baggage?
Remind me of my commitment to embodying courage?

The Art of Raw Desire

Will you be seduced by my charms, what lies on the surface?
Or dive to the depths of our highest purpose?
When I've forgotten my worth and swimming in doubt
Will you remind me what love is really about?
Will you help me find bravery when I'm drowning in fear?
Will you hold my hand and wipe away a tear?
If you see me at my worst, can you see me at my best?
Do you realise I won't settle for anything less?
Will you touch me and tease me till I'm moaning in pleasure?
Will your actions show me I'm the one that you truly treasure?
Will you remember the gift it is to be alive?
Help us both grow and truly thrive
And when you've witnessed every aspect of me,
Will you smile and giggle and let me just be?

The Art of Raw Desire

Poetry & Artwork of Sex, Love & Relationships

Raw Desire

Erupt me into a volcano of volatility, powerful and fierce tearing through the illusion of stability
Fuck me open and leave me in my juices to bathe in the depth of my own waters
Indulge my deepest desires and tantalise me with truths beyond the consciousness of these realms
Teach me the ways of the fearless warrior as I teach you the art of raw desire
Pain. Pleasure. Passion. Power.
Pulsate within me
Dive deep into the mystery of the dark abyss and arise fallen solider into the loving arms of the angels that guide you.
You are safe, you are held, you are loved.

The Art of Raw Desire

Dreaming

Am I awake or asleep?
Diving into the deep
Subconscious realms of symbols and colours
Highlighting the space between us and others
Feeling and knowing the messages shown
Reflecting back how I have grown
Intuition paving the way to action
Showing repulsion and revealing attraction
Emotions dancing within my being
Influencing the way in which I am seeing
The world around me, outside and in
Giving me the courage to begin
The pilgrimage of truth, divine initiation
A message from God, an open invitation
To have faith in the guidance, to believe in the path
To realise this life is just here for a laugh
A communion between myself and Spirit
Stretching me to reach to my limit
Breaking the ego, humbling the mind
Digging deep within to find
The messages held and known all along
That I am safe in this world to belong
To love, to dance, to celebrate all
To stand again after I fall
Held up by the love all around me
Giving me permission to truly be

The Art of Raw Desire

Poetry & Artwork of Sex, Love & Relationships

Magic Moments

My ice cream, my sweet treat
Melting moments as our lips meet
Giggling till sunrise
Dancing with the butterflies
As I find paradise in your arms
Disarmed by your cheeky charms
Our song has the sweetest melody
A duet, a dance, a healing remedy
A tincture for my weary mind
A beauty I had forgotten to find
In each and every changing moment
Life as a friend not opponent
Releasing control, finding my flow
Highlighting where I am still to grow
Knowing my strengths, knowing my weaknesses
Boy my kryptonite is your kisses
Tingles and turn ons
Synchronistic omens
I need help to ground this iconicity
Cause I'm charged up like electricity
Bring me to earth
So I know my worth
Cause the way you look at me
Reminds me to relax and see
There's nowhere to be, nowhere to go
No one to be, nothing to show
Because each moment shared with you
Is a magic moment coming true

The Art of Raw Desire

Rebirth

Dawn breaks on a new day
Fresh eyes with each golden ray
Bringing new perceptions
On lies and deceptions
Truths we hide from the people in our life
Shielding them to avoid inflicting strife
But the stories we tell ourselves are the worst
The ones that undermine our worth
Caught in feelings of never being enough
Thickening our skin to try and keep us tough
Hiding behind masks of approval
Repressing desires deemed unusual
Losing the sparkle in our eye
As a part of us numbs and believes the lie
That the world is supposed to fit in a box
As the shackles stay on and the padlock locks
Surviving not thriving, making it bearable
Moulded to what is perceived as acceptable
Into roles we never intended to live
Where our deepest teaching is to forgive
Ourselves for putting others needs before our own
For believing the thought that we are alone
Denying our desire to truly be held
To dissolve into bliss, as bodies meld
Remembering hope, letting that inner child laugh
As we're guided to our unique and individual path
Messengers reflected in the cycles of the earth
For life is a balance of death and rebirth

The Art of Raw Desire

Poetry & Artwork of Sex, Love & Relationships

The Authentic You

If you don't believe in Magic
Wait till you see her open
When she cries, when she flies
When she moans, when she groans
Hold her softly, hold her tight
For with the wind she will take flight
Run naked with her through fields of gold
This gypsy won't do as she is told
Dance in the winds of mystery
Together rewrite history
Keep her wild and keep her free
This precious beauty was never meant to be
Hidden away be-hind closed doors
Or trapped on land looking out from the shores
Great oceans holding the unknown
Were never meant to be sailed alone
She'll keep you guessing, keep you amused
Maybe even slightly confused

The Art of Raw Desire

Don't try and rationally understand
Just trust in her outstretched hand
Beckoning you to come and play
Listen closely without delay
She'll whisper secrets of the soul
Even when there is no goal
But without the presence of loving eyes
The fire of passion slowly dies
Something sad, something tragic
So look for treasures, look for Magic
For the heart sees beyond it all
In silence hear its gentle call
There's nothing you could say or do
That would change me seeing the authentic you

The Art of Raw Desire

Poetry & Artwork of Sex, Love & Relationships

contemplation

The ultimate truth of contemplation
What is needed for redemption
Are my thoughts real, is my mind a liar?
The bias of pure desire
Are these thoughts of the mind or of the body?
Are they profane or pure and holy?
Am I looking for atonement from my bad deeds
Or innocently asking for my primal needs
Is it yes, is it no
Never clear of where to go
Sitting and listening to the devil inside
Giggling at my cheeky guide
Sense or censor, less or more
What do I truly love and adore?
A gentle touch or simple kiss
The art of desire, eternal bliss
But with light comes dark
A deep bite mark

The Art of Raw Desire

Scratches imprinted on my bare skin
As this game of tease we slowly begin
Knowing the fantasies that live inside
We'll surely be in for an interesting ride
I close my eyes and it all fades away
I've found the way I want to pray
Lay me bare with a stare
Try and match me, if you dare
The fires of my dangerous side
Are not something I'll try and hide
Burning karma, relinquishing armour
With passion and purpose you'll surely disarm her
Corrupt and erupt the silent psyche
Explode and erode so that you can see
The purity and innocence of intimacy
Allowing our sexual nature to be free

The Art of Raw Desire

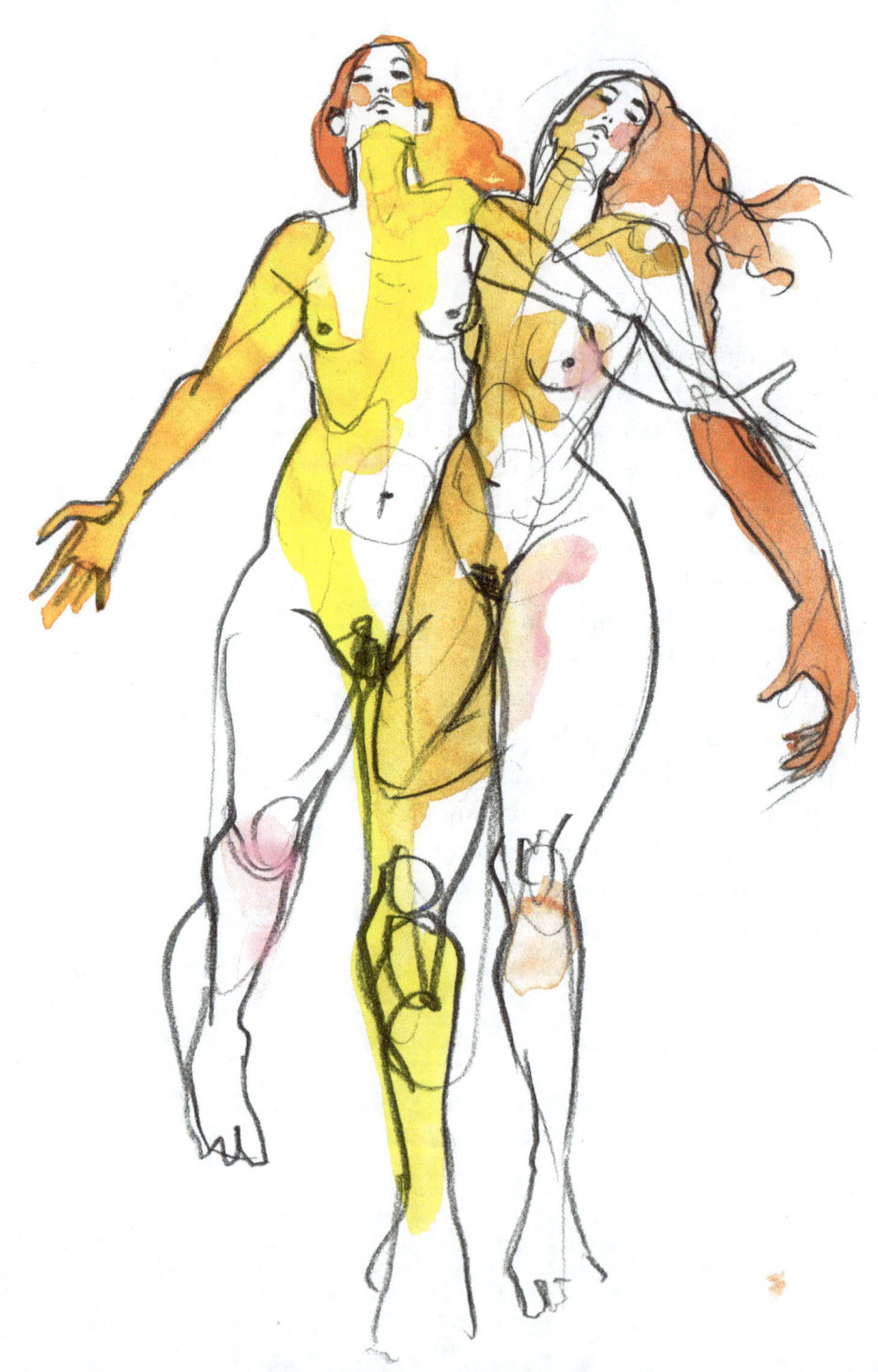

stardust

So she said I'll fly to the moon where I'll dance with the stars
Onwards and upwards on my way to mars
Bathed in the moonlight where I'm held in your arms
Whisked away by your charismatic charms
A shooting star, make a wish
May every moment I can truly cherish
Knowing that things will never last
Stuck in illusions of the past
Seduced by the darkness you draw me out
Into the sunshine so I'm out and about
Frolicking the fields of green and gold
Reminding my child that I'll never get old
Cheeky mischief as it all falls away
Releasing inhibitions and coming out to play
Nothing needed but the now
Being present, just teach me how
To know my strengths, know my power
Pain or pleasure won't make me cower
Being enough, getting it right
Comes when we're willing to give up the fight

The Art of Raw Desire

Of battling the ego, our own little war
Happening inside us, behind a closed door
The medicine of trust, of knowing our worth
Comes when we live in harmony with the earth
The wisdom held within the land
The beauty beneath where we currently stand
A reflection of the relationship held within
That shows us where the healings begin
Instead of escaping to the ether above
Embodying joy, living in love

The Art of Raw Desire

Poetry & Artwork of Sex, Love & Relationships

Crazy About You

I'll confess a sin
All I want to do is let you in
Hold me, scold me
Take me, make me...
Plead for more
I've never been more sure
That I want this, want us
This is more then just lust
You know that it's true
I'm crazy about you
A little obsessed
My mind with no rest
Playing out the fantasy
Of having you next to me
Pick me up and I'll fly
I'm not even going to try
To resist this urge
For our bodies to merge
Close grind
Come inside
Wrap my legs around you
Boy I love what you do
Explore me, adore me
Private tour of my body
Your blowing my mind
A one of a kind
Experience, appearance
Cause you know it's true
I'm crazy about you

The Art of Raw Desire

Poetry & Artwork of Sex, Love & Relationships

Beautiful Mess

If we live and we die
Who really am I?
A constant quest in which I find
I am something beyond this beautiful mind
If I believe in faith and embody hope
I see life through a kaleidoscope
Colourful and vibrant
Inner voice silent
Captured in awe
A life I adore
I am a question with no answer
A delicate dancer
Interweaving it seems
With your hopes and dreams
But don't be deceived
By my attempts to lead
I'm as scared as you
If only you knew

The Art of Raw Desire

I am a beautiful mess and everything in between
But if you are my King, I'll be your Queen
By no means am I perfect but I'll do my best
Humility and courage put to the test
Don't fix me or trick me, I'm a simple soul
Both completely composed and out of control
I won't promise the world but I'll promise you this
I'll love you through the unknown abyss
Don't lead me and don't follow just stay by my side
Hold my hand while we enjoy this ride
I'll melt in your arms if you hold them wide
If you open your heart and let me inside
Let's co-create magic in a beautiful mess
Smile at life as we say yes

The Art of Raw Desire

Rainbows

Colours weaving in the sky
Refracted off droplets way up high
Dancing diamonds in the air
Caught in motion by your stare
Beauty unfolding right before you
Redefining what you thought you knew
The skies hold wisdom beyond the mind
Explore with openness and you will find
Connections written in the stars
Embodied through living avatars
Rainbows leading to unknown gold
Life rewards the brave and bold
Courageous actions guided by the heart
The hero's journey in which to embark
Take the path of least regret
With gratitude for every person you have met
Taking moments as they come
Following the trail of every breadcrumb

The Art of Raw Desire

Jigsaw puzzles that fall into place
Trusting in life's plan, no need to chase
The knowing of what lies beyond the veil
Releasing control of understanding in detail
Why things unfold as they do
Constantly evolving into something new
Don't seek or search for unknown treasure
You'll never find it through what you can measure
Intuition steering, adventures ahoy
Follow the colour, follow your joy
Mysteries lying in the unknown
Follow the rainbow all the way home

The Art of Raw Desire

Poetry & Artwork of Sex, Love & Relationships

Forbidden Fruit

Treading between worlds
Weaving delicate words
Questions perched on the tip of the tongue
Poetry written, melodies sung
Art of hearts
As this romance starts
Forbidden fruit why are you so sweet?
Tingles all over as our lips meet
Why do you not leave my mind?
Keeping me awake with bodies intertwined
Sending me to Eden
No way of leavin'
Caught in delirium
No way to hear them
Whispers of warning
Sends anticipation soaring
Am I sane or insane?
Egocentric or just vain?
Feeling your desire and wanting more
Wanting you to see me bare and raw

The Art of Raw Desire

Hidden truths
Mind based sleuths
Power plays
To keep desires at bay
Deep remembering
Bodies trembling
Ready to let go
Ready to know
How you taste on my lips
How you feel between my hips
Opening Pandora's box
Are you ready for what it unlocks?

The Art of Raw Desire

Tremble

Boy I see you quiver
Does my power make you shiver?
Give me the wheel
And I'll make you feel
Build anticipation
Taking you to pure elation
Sweet surrender, let go
I know that you know
But I'll confess my sins
Bad intentions is where it begins
My body screaming out
Penetrating through any doubt
Come closer and feel my fire
As I fuel your desire
Curse or cure?
If intentions are pure
I'll take what I need
Let my animal feed
Take me, shake me, break me open
Tremble. Tremble. Release.

The Art of Raw Desire

Poetry & Artwork of Sex, Love & Relationships

claim

My wild animal you can only tame
If you're willing to truly claim
Every aspect of your power
Otherwise my strength will make you cower
Make a stand for what is yours
Take bold steps fiercely towards
The ideas that make you come alive
The dreams that help you truly thrive
Magnetic allure drawing you in
I'll patiently wait with a cheeky grin
Serenade my soul, win me over
Guide out bodies to come in closer
I'll test and challenge your dedication
To lay the grounds for a firm foundation
If you capture me, if your mission succeeds
I'll fill your world with dirty deeds
I'll reward your efforts with adorning affection
Worship your body's pulsating erection
I won't pretend and I will not hide
That I want you within me deep inside
I know there's a choice of which wolf we feed
So I'll wait for you to take the lead
Let you break down every wall
Have you catch me when I fall
You know I want you but I need to see
That you can step up, take over and claim me
You don't need my permission or to approve
Of what you do just make your move
If I seem like an endless riddle
Then meet me, greet me, in the middle

The Art of Raw Desire

Green Eyes

Stepping stones to treasures unknown
Trust in the guidance that is shown
There's always more than meets the eye
Words behind her every sigh
Moans of love making remedies
Sweet silence between the melodies
Can you hold her when she's raw, open, tender?
Allow her to let go, complete surrender
Slowly revealing layer by layer
The truths and secrets that build her, make her
Jigsaw puzzles that piece together
Her inner workings, her hidden pleasure
A work of art, a mystical muse
A game you can never win or lose
The beauty standing before you now
Will whisper secrets to teach you how
To untether the wild spirit held within
Will give you clues on where to begin
To take her to places beyond her dreams
Teasing, tantalising till she screams
The beauty in the storm as you let her unfold
Do you hear what is said between what you're told?
Do you feel her defences dissolve when you're near?
As she gives over control, she lets you steer
A whole new world just with you
Redefining what she thought was always true
Magic carpet rides through diamond skies
The raw desire behind emerald green eyes

The Art of Raw Desire

Poetry & Artwork of Sex, Love & Relationships

Dawn Break

A new moment, a new day
Breaking the horizon with a single ray
Memorised by the light dancing on the ocean
Drawing me in with her enticing potion
Washing me clean and holding me in
Perfect day in which to begin
With a breath of fresh air
Jumping in if you dare
To her watery depths, her deeper knowing
The clarity in which she's showing
That this is no ordinary day, a special occurrence
Synchronicities heightened for reassurance
Messages from the ones above
Loyalty to eternal love
Breath-taking moments to nurture faith
Showing me that love really can be safe
Each moment capturing unique beauty
With each and every emotion truly...
Unveiling gratitude for being alive
So standing by the ocean I jump in, I dive.

The Art of Raw Desire

Poetry & Artwork of Sex, Love & Relationships

Inhale. Exhale.

Inhale. Exhale.
Breathe me in.
Dissolve into the space between our bodies.
Merge with the urge.
Melt into the longing.

Ignite and unite.
Inhale. Exhale.
Breathe me in.
Lose yourself in the ecstasy of elation.
Corrupt and erupt.
The passion of fire.
Arousing desire.

Inhale. Exhale.
Breathe me in.
Move with the waters, the ebb and flow.
Crash into me.
Wash over me.
Sink to the depths.

The Art of Raw Desire

Inhale. Exhale.
Breathe me in.
Get drunk on the intoxicating swirl of emotion.
Surrender to love.
The motion of devotion.
Intertwine with the divine.

Inhale. Exhale.
Breathe me in.
Inhale. Exhale.

Breathe me in.

The Art of Raw Desire

Rainclouds

Teasing and tantalising the solid earth with the moisture of her loins
Dancing droplets dripping from her darkness meeting the ground with a sweet kiss
Drowning the parched lands with the waters of heaven
Soothing the cracks caused by harsh and hardening climates
Dissolving dryness into wet lands
Fertile grounds for endless possibilities
A home for new sprouts, new ideas
Oozing with the prospect of abundance
Death and rebirth
A balancing act between withholding and saturating
Fertile soils turning to mud with the overflow of her juices
The fine line between growth and destruction
For with her outpour and thunderstorms comes suffocation
Drowning the seeds in her depth
Knowing the inherent strength of plants to grow when gives space
She listens and waits
Mother nature's infinite wisdom
Knowing the interplay of nurture and nature
The timing of her gifts
The power of her teachings
The potency of her waters.

The Art of Raw Desire

Poetry & Artwork of Sex, Love & Relationships

shipwreck

You had the courage to lose track of the shore
But the pain of the past burnt to the core
The skeletons lying at the bottom of the ocean
Stirred with the turmoil of upheaving emotion
The masts were sturdy and the bow was strong
But when the storms came something went wrong
And down to the bottom of the waters she fell
Without a word, a scream or a yell
The lady of the ocean buried beneath
A smile of knowing, pearly white teeth
The familiar depths of the waters below
This world was her home, her place to go
Away from the distractions of wild commotion
Back to the truth of raw devotion
A place to listen, reflect and pray
To allow her wary mind to lay
When the storms above thrashed and bellowed
Her attention and focus immediately narrowed
To the calling to withdraw into the self
To return to her vitality, healing and health
A goodbye kiss, a final breath
The ship returned to the beauty of the depth
A shipwreck at the bottom of the sea
Was finally given permission to be.

The Art of Raw Desire

Poetry & Artwork of Sex, Love & Relationships

completion

After the fall
Under it all
You may discover
I'm an angel undercover
I won't save you
Or try to tame you
I'll just sit and smile
While I watch your denial
I can never change
Or rearrange
The way things are
So I'll love from a far
At times we must face
What we try and chase
Share our truth
Without the sleuth
To pave the way
For a clearer day
Where we all can be free
And give space to be
Perfectly raw
So we can soar
Now I must go
I know it is so
After the fun
Our time is done
I'll leave you better then when I found you
I hope that one day you'll see it to be true

The Art of Raw Desire

wings

My teachers hidden in cloaks of deceit
Orchestrated to bring me to my feet
Bowing to the grace of the unknown
Praying for guidance to be shown
Reflecting patterns of human nature
That in myself I don't wish to nurture
Reminding me to look within
To find the places in which to bring
The nurturing intention of love and forgiveness
Towards my unquestionable human-ness
Knowing my limitations, owning my fears
Then clarity on the road suddenly appears
Back to the home within the heart
Out of the mind that keeps us apart
Lover or enemy, friend or foe
To what honour do I owe
Each person within my precious life
That gives me love or causes me strife
A guest with a unique and special gift
Some that drop and some that lift
No right or wrong, less or more
Just messengers to bring me to my core
Of what I desire and aspire to be
Of what in the world I wish to see
Trust the path, aim for the sky
Find my wings and see me fly

The Art of Raw Desire

grey

What do we do when we sit in the grey
What do we share when there's no words to say
Helpless or hopeful it's all in the mind
Look inside and you'll know what to find
The truth of it all is we're doing our best
Stumbling in the dark gambling on a guess
Nothing in life is ever guaranteed
Numbness or pain if emotions aren't freed
Tripping on words when I don't know what to do
Trying to find clarity when there's a storm cloud to walk through
Life laughs when things don't fit in a box
When we have to choose to remove our own locks
I constantly find myself outside the lines
Having to trust in following the signs
The delicate weavings that led me to you
You smiled at me when you realised I knew
But with expectations I'll crumble to pieces
Locked in old patterns as freedom decreases
Confined by the thoughts of right or wrong
Trying to find out where I exactly belong

The Art of Raw Desire

I can't deny, I have to admit
In your arms is where I most want to fit
I'm perfectly me, human and all
And even when strong I'll inevitably fall
But when I'm with you I giggle inside
Laughter is something I just can't hide
You light up my world, in a corny way
Remind me of the importance of childlike play
Your dorky jokes and smooth mishaps
Gets me thinking that maybe, perhaps
I need to reassess what life's really about
If caught in an illusion of fear & doubt
We can't embrace life in all its expressions
So surround yourself with people that leave lasting impressions
The ones that make you feel warm and fuzzy within
Where you can't hold back a cheesy grin
Know your worth, stand for your needs
And fill your life with thoughtful deeds
What you give out comes back around
Discover the pot of gold you really have found
For without the grey on a clear, bright day
The rainbows are hidden far away
Embrace the beauty of what is seen
And love the shades that fall in between

The Art of Raw Desire

Poetry & Artwork of Sex, Love & Relationships

I Choose You

Melting moments dripping from my lips
Juices flowing from between my hips
The taste of desire lingers in the air
Feeling the potency of your stare
Seeing and reading between the lines
A delicate skill of sensing the signs
Caressing and holding me in your embrace
Slowing me down from this crazy rat race
Pouring deep truth into my soul
Reminding me of the collective whole
I sense your strength, I feel your power
My emotional storms won't make you cower
In any situation you'll try and stand tall
Dedicated to the task of not letting me fall
My fearless warrior, your disarming temptress
Dissolving your armour, removing my black dress
Rewriting the fears engrained in our psyche
Heightening senses living inside me
Scratch down the walls constraining this being
Remove the conditioning that stops me from seeing
Erotic blueprints carved into my skin
As you move inside me, I let you in
Not just my body but mind and heart
This dance of devotion a pure form of art
Is this how effortless things are meant to be?
Is this what it's meant to feel like to be free?
The intricate signs that led me to you
My belief and faith are shining through
Trusting the guidance from above
Is making me consider that I think this is love.

The Art of Raw Desire

what If

What if I fall and you don't catch me?
If you feel trapped and not free
What if I can't be what you thought?
If I'm not everything that you sought
What if you feel like you're not enough?
If I push you away to try and stay tough
What if I can't keep your attention?
If I get bitter from your wandering affection
What if it's not the right timing?
If mistrust becomes controlling
What if I start asking for too much?
If you feel overwhelmed and run from my touch
What if we don't communicate what we're really feeling?
If we block the opportunity for truly healing
What if we freeze and both get scared?
If the load feels heavy instead of shared
What if I can't tell you that I don't know what to do?
If you misinterpret my silence as rejection towards you
What if we're caught in limbo with no way out?
If we stay in loops analysing our doubt

The Art of Raw Desire

But then a little voice whispers inside,
That maybe this is something I shouldn't hide…

What if we try and we actually fly?
If we're left in an intoxicating, natural high
What if reality exceeds expectations?
If we explore the depth of our imaginations
What if indulging our desires brings unspeakable pleasure?
If it goes above and beyond what we can rationally measure
What if I let these juices flow like an endless river?
If I give my body permission to deeply quiver
What if to you my cum tastes like heaven?
If on a scale of one to ten, I rate you eleven
What if we inspire each other to be the best we can be?
If we choose to explore the possibility
That this joy and happiness could continue to grow?
If we release the 'what if…' and give it a go

The Art of Raw Desire

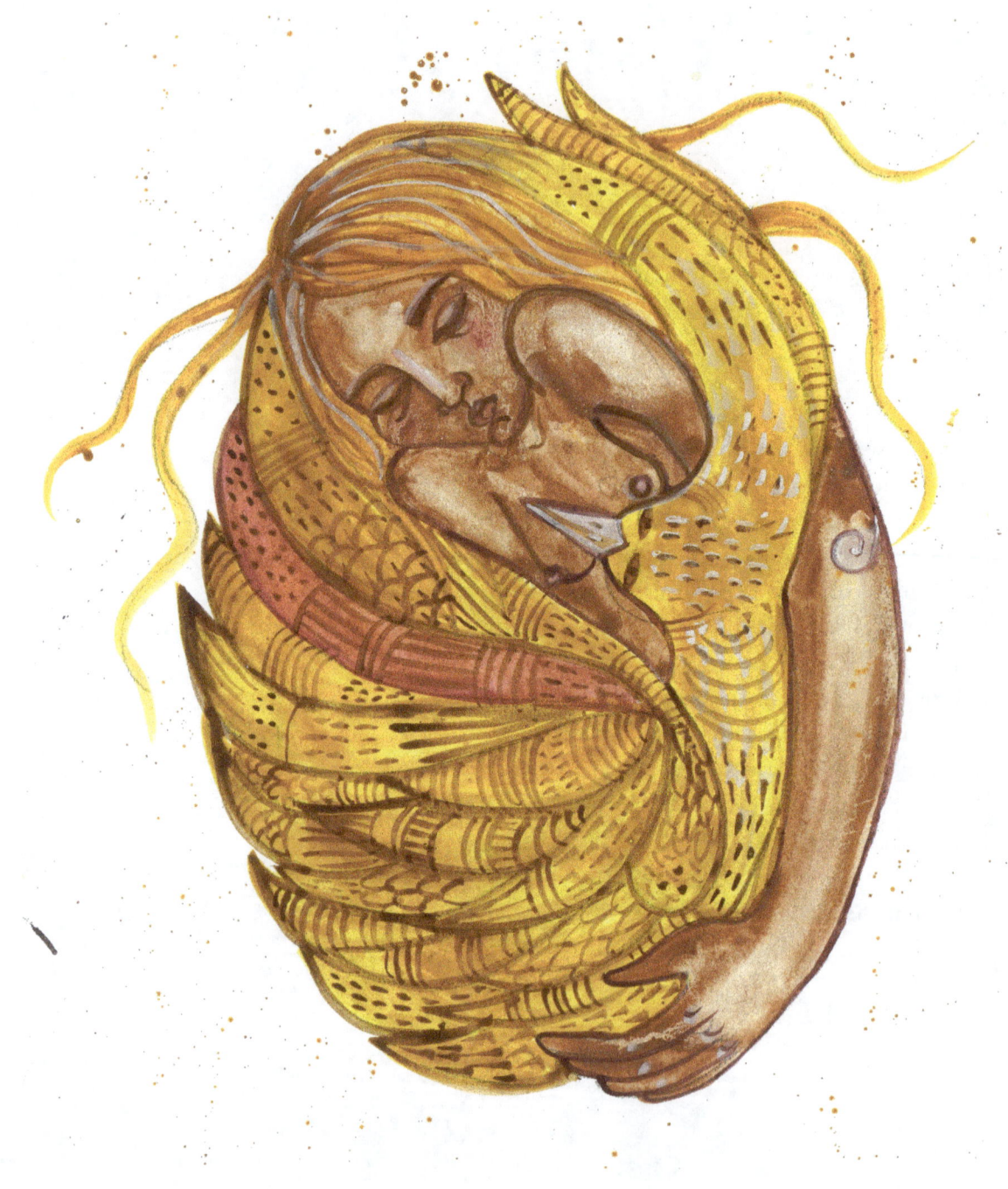

Poetry & Artwork of Sex, Love & Relationships

vows to Oneself

My beloved, this is my promise to you
To allow my devotion for you to cut through
The illusion of doubt, fear and separation
To penetrate with love, in pure elation
You are my inspiration, my mystical beauty
My muse to life, my one and truly
I promise to make you laugh when I make mistakes
I promise to hold you tightly when your tender heart aches
I promise to love you the best way I know how
To be present and true to the here and now
A promise from my heart to love you as you are
Even in your darkness you are my brightest star
Your beautiful flaws, imperfect perfections
Gives my energetic cock real big erections
You're the sweetest song I could ever sing
My constant reminder that the universe is always listening
To the greatest desire of my soul
To be united with my beloved, to feel whole
You are my one and only, my greatest blessing
So with a vow of love and devotion I give you this ring
As a reminder of our union and commitment to self
To hold you forever and put you above all else
I love you my darling always and forever
Never apart, always together

The Art of Raw Desire

Dr. Jae West, PhD

Jae West uses words and rhymes to take readers on a journey into the realms of imagination. Interweaving passion and playfulness she explores the themes of sex, love and relationships to connect people to a shared sense of excitement for life. Her poems draw from real life experience, reflecting the depths and magic of falling in love, both with another and oneself. Her poems are an ode to the beauty that arises from loving oneself and vulnerability of speaking one's truth, connecting readers to the inner smile of the heart. Jae is from Western Australia, and is a dancer, performer, PhD graduate, yoga teacher, and student of life.

@jae_west4

Kate Gillett

Kate Gillett uses art as a medium to explore life's journey. Her work expands across many mediums, and has common themes of symbolism, womanhood, eros and befriending the shadows. She has found great meaning in the way art lives on through other people's stories and interpretation as it is released into the world. Combining her work with poetry written by others gives Kate's work new life and energy. Kate is from Western Australia, and is a mother, dancer, lover of nature and student of Creative Arts Psychotherapy.

@kate.gillett

The Art of Raw Desire

Poetry & Artwork of Sex, Love & Relationships

www.ingramcontent.com/pod-product-compliance
Lightning Source LLC
Chambersburg PA
CBHW060304010526
44108CB00042B/2674